IMAGES
of England

ENGLISH
ELECTRIC

W.E.W. 'Teddy' Petter, eccentric but brilliant designer of the Lightning and Canberra.

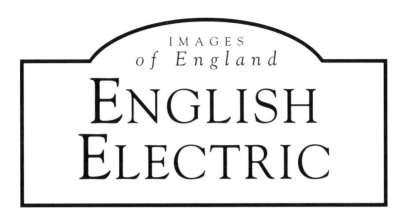

IMAGES
of England

ENGLISH
ELECTRIC

Compiled by
Derek N. James

TEMPUS

First published 1999
Copyright © Derek N. James, 1999

Tempus Publishing Limited
The Mill, Brimscombe Port,
Stroud, Gloucestershire, GL5 2QG

ISBN 0 7524 1178 0

Typesetting and origination by
Tempus Publishing Limited
Printed in Great Britain by
Midway Clark Printing, Wiltshire

Published to commemorate the 50th Anniversary of the first flight of the Canberra, *English Electric's first jet aircraft, on Friday 13 May 1949.*

Lightning F1s of No 74 Squadron, Royal Air Force, in an immaculate
starboard echelon formation.

Contents

Acknowledgements

One of my early tasks in Gloster Aircraft Company's Sales Office was replying to requests for data and photographs of the Meteor jet fighter. One small Dutch boy got his wires crossed in 1949 when he wrote to Gloster asking for photographs of 'the new English A1 electric bomber and the batteries which powered it'! His letter was redirected to Preston. This was my first contact with the English Electric Company.

The Concise Oxford Dictionary lists 32 words with the prefix 'photo' which stems from the Greek *photos* – meaning 'light'. The word of most importance to this book is 'photograph'. Without them it would tell only a small part of the life story of this great aircraft manufacturer whose roots are deep in the soil of Northwest Lancashire. Among those people who have kindly loaned me photographs I am particularly grateful to Brian Tomlinson of British Aerospace Northwest Heritage Group who spent many hours searching for photographs and answering endless questions about English Electric and all its works; to Louise Weymouth and Joanne Ichimura, archivists at GEC-Marconi's Research Centre, who dug deeply to find photographs and historical details of the five companies which were to form the English Electric Company Ltd; to Mike Hooks who, once again, lent me rare photographs from his fine collection; to John Squier, formerly English Electric's chief production test pilot and to his daughter Junie Arnold. Others who came to my aid were Clifford Walter Bateson, Sally Bradford, W G Brooks, Ronald Byrom, Colin Charnley, Ruth Cornwell, Leslie Coombs, Gwilym Davies, Dale Donovan (Command Public Relations Officer, RAF Strike Command), Judith Donovan and Kay Lewis (Judith Donovan Associates), Keith Emslie, Robert Fairclough, Harry Holmes, Bernice Howlett, Ian Lawrenson, Stuart Leslie, Alex Lumsden, Alan McKnight (Short Brothers' Visual Communications Manager), Norman Parker, David Pratt, N C Watts, Jack Wilcock, John Williams (Archivist, Willans Works, Rugby), Kenneth Wixey and Harry Woodman.

For their continuing advice, patience and good humour I thank those members of the Tempus Publishing team who consistently turn my sows' ears into silken purses. My thanks go yet again to my wife, Brenda, whose skill and speed at the controls of our PC persuaded 15,861 words to join the other one on the floppy disc before the Millennium Bug got its teeth into them.

DNJ
Barnwood, Gloucester
February 1999

One

It was all Wright in the Beginning

Did you know that the Wright Brothers were English and that the first aeroplane they built, in 1907, was a helicopter? No! Not Orville and Wilbur! *These* Wright brothers were Howard T., a mechanical and electrical engineer, with Walter S. and Warwick J. who were into motor cars.

Howard T. (it stood for 'Theophilus') did his engineering training in his father's Tipton factory in Staffordshire. Then, the quietly spoken young Howard, sporting a fashionable waxed moustache, began working for the US-born Hiram Maxim (of the revolutionary quick-firing gun) at Baldwyns Park, Bexley in Kent. Maxim had patented 'a lightweight steam aero-engine' and 'a basic flying machine, mounted on rails with a retaining rail above'. He also modified the 'roundabouts' device created by his compatriot Samuel Langley for experimental 'flying' and began his own aerodynamic experiments. While Langley swung small models around a 12ft circle, Maxim 'flew' much larger wings around a 1,000ft circumference. This work fired Howard's interest in aviation.

When Maxim's company closed its doors in 1904, the Wright brothers pooled their aviation, electrical and motor car knowledge and formed the Howard T. Wright Brothers business.

One day, a letter addressed to Maxim suddenly landed on Howard Wright's desk. An Italian, Fredrico Capone, had designed a twin-rotor helicopter/glider and was looking for someone to build it. Wright jumped at the chance to get back into aeronautics. After construction in the Wrights' Battersea workshop in 1908 and some brief flight tests, which proved that it was too heavy and under-powered, the helicopter was despatched to Italy. Capone then designed a very similar aeroplane of half the weight with increased wingspan and improved rotors which was also built by Wright. This was flown successfully in Britain before delivery. The flight profile would have been similar to that of a wood pigeon; rising with increased rotor revolutions and then gliding and falling when the power was cut!

Thus, the first and possibly the most important aviation element of the ultimately pentagonal-shaped foundations of English Electric's aviation interests was laid. Now – who were the five 'foundationers'? Alphabetically they were the Coventry Ordnance Works Ltd (COW); Dick, Kerr & Company; Phoenix Dynamo Manufacturing Company; the United Electric Car Company and Willans & Robinson Ltd. Their products were all connected with electrical engineering, power generation and electrically propelled vehicles of different kinds.

COW's forerunner was Mulliners, Birmingham coachbuilders who turned to building big guns for the Army and Navy. Dick, Kerr & Co. in Glasgow was into everything from electric traction, civil engineering and railway electrical systems to boats, cattle-weighing machines and tramcars. The trams were built in Preston by a subsidiary, Electric Railway and Tramway Carriage Works (ERTCW) which was formed in 1898. A near neighbour was the English

Electric Manufacturing Co. Ltd, engaged in similar electrical work. About five years later, after a period of what was described as 'intimate collaboration' between these two companies, Dick, Kerr bought English Electric Manufacturing; it also changed the name of ERTCW to the United Electric Car Co Ltd. (UECC). Another Bradford electrical engineering business with links to these two companies was Phoenix Dynamo Manufacturing Co. The fifth element of English Electric's pentagonal foundations was forecast when a Phoenix generator installation was powered by a Willans & Robinson engine built in Rugby.

While these organisations were each beavering away in there own specialised industry, Howard T. Wright, was quietly planning to design, build and modify aeroplanes for a number of pioneering aeronauts. In this work he was greatly aided by the ginger-haired, bespectacled William O. Manning who joined Wright as his designer in 1908. For a few brief years these two spearheaded their small company's business, which earned fame as Britain's leading aircraft builder.

Howard T.'s first job after Capone's helicopter was at Brooklands installing a 24hp French Buchet engine in John Moore-Brabazon's own design biplane glider built by the Short brothers. Howard also repositioned the forward elevator on outriggers and modified the tail unit. However, the lack of power was a major contributor to its undoing. 'Brab' commented that the four-wheeled undercarriage was 'weak and flabby', adding that he 'hadn't tried any experiments with it while running down the race track' – probably because the track's manager was not too pleased at its use for testing aeroplanes! Subsequently, 'Brab' removed the engine and flew his aeroplane as a kite. With a 35ft wingspan this must have been a difficult device to handle.

Beginning with a biplane for Malcolm Seton-Karr, Wright produced a number of aircraft, mostly designed by himself and Manning, for enthusiasts and syndicates who had the money but not the facilities or skills to do so themselves. He also expanded his little company, buying sheds at Brooklands, Eastchurch and Larkhill. Things were humming along nicely. However, the bubble was about to burst.

The year 1911 marked a decline in the Company's fortunes. Despite his 44 years, Howard was still rather diffident about his accomplishments. Perhaps he had 'run out of steam' or had some private disagreement with Manning. Whatever, he cashed in a large chunk of his Warwick Wright Ltd shares, sold his aviation interests to Coventry Ordnance Works – where he worked briefly – .then moved to the Isle of Wight.

Meanwhile, Manning's move to COW as chief designer came at a most opportune moment. On 13 May 1911 the Royal Flying Corps and its Naval Wing were officially inaugurated. Then, in December, the War Office announced a competition at Larkhill on Salisbury Plain to choose the aeroplanes for the British Army's Air Battalion. This competition became known as the 'Military Aircraft Trials', with a main prize of £4,000. The initial aim was to provide the RFC with a standard reconnaissance aeroplane, following the Army's adoption of a standard rifle, field gun and other equipment. Large orders were anticipated for the winning design.

Manning rapidly designed two biplanes. One had a 100hp French Gnome rotary engine, twin fins and rudders and side-by-side seating while a French 110hp Chenu in-line, water-cooled engine powered the other one which had tandem cockpits. In April 1912 the first aircraft was flight tested at Brooklands by Tommy Sopwith, COW's test pilot. The Gnome-engined aeroplane handled quite well but its engine and chain drive to the propeller gave constant trouble. The Chenu engine in the second aircraft was problem-ridden and is reported as 'practically failing to run at all'. Neither aircraft were exactly star turns. Both failed to complete several of the Trials' stages; so it was back to the drawing board for Manning and COW. The story of the Military Trials is not for these pages; suffice it to say that the BE.2 biplane, largely designed by Geoffrey de Havilland and built by the Royal Aircraft Factory at Farnborough, was the winner - even though it wasn't admitted as an official entrant. This was because one of the judges, the monocled, flamboyant but keen-brained Mervyn O'Gorman, was the Factory's Superintendent. Indirectly, COW benefited from this exercise. When the developed BE.2a and 2b were ordered in 1914, COW built a small number.

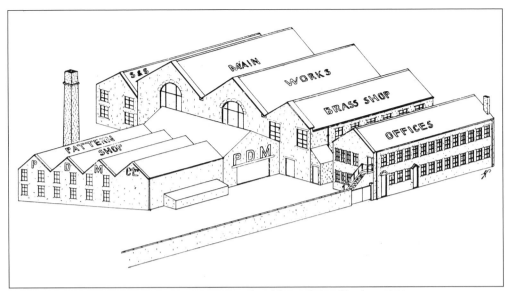

Drawing of Phoenix Dynamo's factory on Leeds Old Road, Bradford in 1903…

…and a photograph of the factory several years later. Buildings shown in the drawing can be identified. The 'Sunday-best' dress of the men and the boy on the bicycle, plus flags, may indicate this is a special day.

Clearly, 'watching the birdie' was no laughing matter for some serious-faced Phoenix Dynamo employees in 1905. The man furthest right smokes a clay-pipe, the tallest in the centre back row, a cigarette – which were five a penny!

West Strand Road, Preston at noon *c.*1902. Workers leave Dick, Kerr & Co.'s Electric Railway &Tramway Carriage Works on the right and English Electric Manufacturing Co. on the left.

Dick, Kerr seemed to be into every branch of engineering in the early 1900s. This was one of six different types of riverboat built for home markets and for export.

Coupling this Willans and Robinson central-valve engine to a Phoenix Dynamo Manufacturing Co.'s 240kW generator in 1903 was instrumental in linking two of the companies which would eventually become part of the English Electric Company.

'Intimate business relations existed between English Electric Manufacturing Co. and Electric Railway & Tramway Carriage Works on either side of Strand Road' according to this 1904 photograph's original caption. It shows 'chippies' at work building wooden tram bodies.

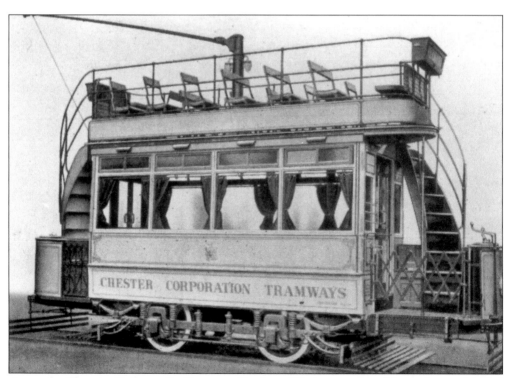

An early Electric Railway & Tramcar Carriage Works tramcar. Note the unshielded motorman's position exposing him to wind and rain, and the 'toast-rack' seats on the open upper deck.

Howard Theophilus Wright, engineer and aviation pioneer, whose aeroplanes built during 1907-1911 laid the first foundations on which the aviation interests of English Electric and its successors were built.

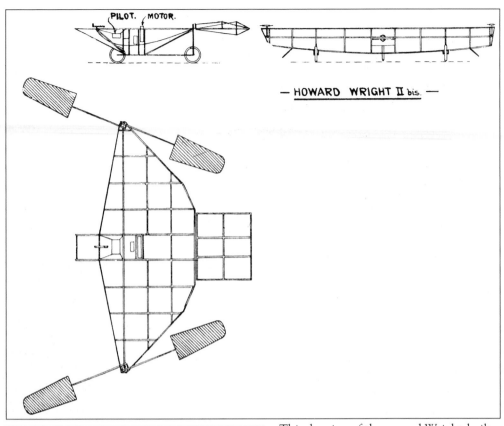

— HOWARD WRIGHT II bis. —

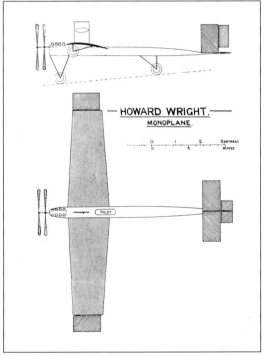

HOWARD WRIGHT.
MONOPLANE.

This drawing of the second Wright-built Capone helicopter/glider with a 30hp REP engine, shows the delta-shaped wing, tip-mounted rotors and general layout. It weighed only 600lb without the pilot.

Designed by Horatio Barber and built by Howard Wright, this two-seat monoplane underwent a number of modifications during its life. Note the contra-rotating propellers and rotating wingtips.

The same monoplane with a second tail-plane behind the pilot, enclosed fuselage and redesigned tail unit.

Howard T. Wright's 1909 biplane built for Malcolm Seton-Karr. It had a 26hp Metallurgique water-cooled engine driving counter-rotating pusher propellers and was 43ft long, with 40ft span wings. Its bicycle landing gear with wing-tip balancing wheels was fifty-one years ahead of the Harrier! Total weight was 1,100lb and area of 'supporting' surfaces was 520 square feet.

In 1910 Howard Wright and Oke Manning built this canard-configured pusher-engine monoplane for the Aeronautical Syndicate Ltd which designed it. The Syndicate was managed by Horation Barber.

Designed by W O Manning, one of the Coventry Ordnance Works' entries for the 1912 Military Aircraft Trials at Larkhill, Salisbury Plain, No.10 had side-by-side seating and a 100hp French Gnome rotary engine.

An extremely rare photograph of Tommy Sopwith flying COW's No.10 Military Trials aircraft. The 2:1 ratio chain drive from the engine can be seen as a 'V' below the propeller spinner.

The 110hp French in-line Chenu engine was loath to run in this second Manning-designed Military Trials aircraft, No.11, that had tandem cockpits and a four-blade propeller.

Ten-and-a-half members of Willans and Robinson's football team of 1914 complete with Association and Rugby Football goal posts. John Whittaker Collier is fourth from left and his brother Thomas is fourth from right.

Two

The War
to End Wars?

When the First World War began on 4 August 1914, hundreds of engineering and woodworking companies stopped making peacetime products and switched to 'munitions', including aeroplanes. COW was already preparing to produce a batch of BE.8as. Before COW's aircraft department closed in 1919, the Company had built some 600 aeroplanes of six different types and sub-types designed by the Royal Aircraft Factory for the Royal Flying Corps, as well as 150 Sopwith Snipes for the still infant Royal Air Force.

Willans & Robinson (W&R) in Rugby, one of English Electric's 'foundationers', was also ahead of the game (a young man named Geoffrey de Havilland, a student with the company during 1905-1909 would make his name in aviation a decade later). In about March 1914 it began planning to produce aero-engines under sub-licence from the Dudbridge Iron Works in Stroud, Gloucestershire. Dudbridge had a licence from Emile Salmson's small Paris-based company to build its radial engines. As beginners in the aero-engine business it couldn't have been easy for W&R to cut their teeth on Salmsons. Not only did they embody the fairly complex Canton-Unne system, in which all the connecting rods drove a cage revolving on the crank-pin on epicyclic gears, but also they were water-cooled. During 1915-1916 W&R built 36 twin-row, 14 cylinder, 200hp 2M-7 engines plus 106 single row, 9 cylinder, 130hp M-9 engines and one experimental engine in 1916-1917. During the latter half of the War, W&R also produced some 220 Sunbeam in-line engines designed by Frenchman Louis Coatalen. Early in April 1915 Prime Minister David Lloyd George had announced in Parliament that, contrary to popular belief, the War would *not* be over by Christmas and that there was a grave shortage of suitable armaments and equipment with which to win it. He called for immediate action to remedy this. Both COW and Willans & Robinson were already helping to close the gap, closely followed by Dick, Kerr and Phoenix Dynamo.

Despite this challenging task, Dick, Kerr pursued its pre-war expansion programme. During 1916-1917 it gained control of Willans & Robinson, (which lacked 'a vigilant and prudent financial policy' although good at design and manufacturing) and the United Electric Car Co which was preparing to build components for Felixstowe F.3 and F.5 flying boats for the Royal Naval Air Service. The hulls were produced by established boat-builders, but Dick, Kerr built the remainder of the structure at Preston before transporting them to South Shields, County Durham for assembly, testing and delivery to East Coast RNAS bases.

Dick, Kerr's last main aviation work was producing major components and final assembly of the first of three giant Atalanta class flying-boats designed by the Fairey Aviation Company to meet the 1917 Admiralty N.4 Specification. The 140ft span (well, 139ft to be honest) and 66ft length of these Atalantas, which made them the world's largest flying boats of that time, were too big for Fairey's factories at Hayes and Harlington in Middlesex, so most of their structure was sub-contracted to other companies. The flexible Linton-Hope hull for the first aircraft

N119, *Atalanta,* was built by May, Harden and May at Hythe. Final assembly began in 1919 at Dick, Kerr's new facility at Lytham. However, *Atalanta* was not completed until 1921 when it was taken to the Marine Aircraft Experimental Unit (MAEU) on the Isle of Grain, Kent. It was re-assembled – but didn't fly until 4 July 1923. This ended Dick, Kerr's aircraft work.

Following Prime Minister Lloyd George's 'call to arms' by British industries, Phoenix Dynamo was one of five companies which, early in 1915, each received orders for twelve Short 184 patrol floatplanes urgently needed by the RNAS. But Shorts had jumped the gun a bit. The prototypes hadn't flown and production drawings were not complete. So each company sent a draughtsman to Shorts' Rochester factory to measure and make 'from life' drawings of the prototypes' components, an early example of today's 'reverse engineering'. The first Phoenix-built floatplane was delivered on 12 January 1916. During the next two years Phoenix built fifty improved Dover-type Short 184s.

Like most manufacturers, Phoenix Dynamo had manpower problems when Territorial Army and other reservists were called up for the Services. But even then these men couldn't escape contact with their peacetime work. One employee who tested dynamos, joined the Royal Navy. When his ship was torpedoed he was picked up by another ship which was immediately sunk by the same German U-boat. Safe aboard another ship, this U-boat claimed its third victim and the man found himself in the water yet again. He was fished out by a Royal Navy cruiser and taken to its engine room for warmth. The first thing he saw was a Phoenix dynamo which he later discovered he had tested in Bradford!

Early in 1918, Phoenix built half a dozen Short Bombers. Although only single-engined their wings, which folded, spanned an enormous 84ft. More rewarding was an order for Maurice Farman S.7 Longhorn trainer aircraft. The exact number built and delivered is open to question but about thirty were ordered. During 1917-1918, Phoenix Dynamo built two unusual Armstrong Whitworth FK.10 quadruplane two-seat fighters and began producing seventy-five Felixstowe F.3 and forty-five F.5 flying boats designed by Lieutenant Commander John Porte. Porte had been invalided out of the Royal Navy with tuberculosis in 1911 but was to continue designing a range of flying boats until he died in 1919.

Building other people's aeroplanes was not enough for Phoenix Dynamo and W.O. Manning, whose persistence paid off when one of his project designs was turned into hardware. This was the P.5 experimental twin-engine, biplane flying boat which was intended as a successor to the Felixstowe 'boats. Armed with five .303in Lewis guns in the hull, one P.5 had two more gun positions in small 'fighting tops' in the upper wings. Occupants of these often suffered from isolation and motion sickness brought on by their 'unusual movements'. Two prototypes were built during 1918-1919. Despite lengthy development with three variants, now designated the Cork I, II and III, none entered production. Nevertheless, as will be seen, they formed the basis for yet another flying boat.

Royal Flying Corps men watch the pilot embark in a COW BE2a - with its engine running - of No.4 Squadron with the British Expeditionary Force in France during August 1914.

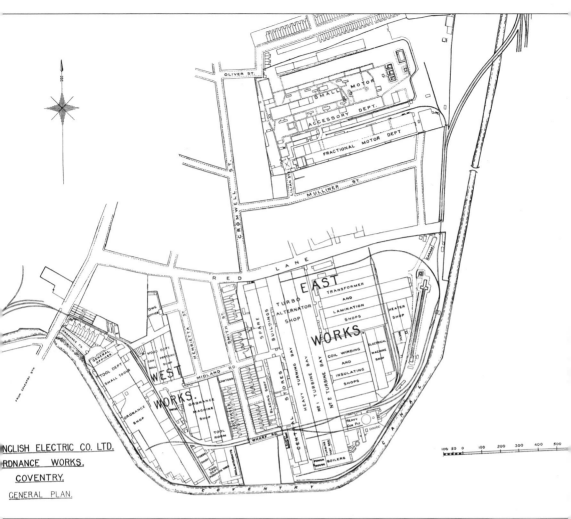

General plan of the Coventry Ordnance Works during the First World War. The main East and West Works are at the bottom of the plan with the smaller Fuze Factory at the top.

The first COW-built BE.8a, 2154, reconnaissance/bomber seen at the Royal Aircraft Factory, Farnborough in 1915. The BE.8a was dubbed the 'Bloater' in RFC service because of its bulbous nose enclosing the Gnome rotary engine.

This single-engine Short Bomber, 9834, was one of six built by Phoenix during the autumn of 1916. The bomber's wings, which could fold, spanned 84ft - that's 15ft more than a twin-engine Hampden of the Second World War.

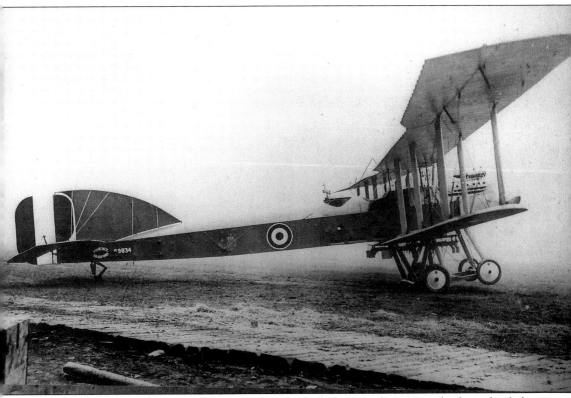

As well as its wide span wings the Short Bomber also had a long fuselage. Note the four-wheeled landing gear, twin open cockpits and the large fin and inset rudder.

This BE.12 reconnaissance/bomber, built by COW during 1916-1917, is pictured at Cramlington, Northumberland while serving with No.58 Squadron. A camera is visible beside the cockpit.

One of COW's six BE.12a conversions at the Aeroplane Experimental Establishment, Martlesham Heath. Its serial number on the fin is displayed as A'597. Note the camera on the port side.

A French 135hp Salmson water-cooled radial engine described as being the first built under licence by Willans & Robinson in Rugby during 1916. It was fitted in a Royal Flying Corps Farman F27 aircraft in India in 1916.

Maurice Farman S7s under construction in Phoenix Dynamo's Bradford factory during 1917.

A French Maurice Farman S7 trainer of which some thirty were produced by Phoenix Dynamo. Its long curving fore-plane structure earned it the unofficial British name of 'the Longhorn'.

The flying venetian blind. Phoenix built two Armstrong Whitworth FK.10 Quadruplanes in 1917. Designed by the Dutchman Fritz Koolhoven the FK.10's four wings enhanced climb performance and handling.

Men and girls busy building N1636, a Dover-type Short 184 torpedo/bomber floatplane at Phoenix Dynamo's factory in 1917.

One of about sixty Phoenix Short 184s at Royal Naval Air Station Cattewater, (later re-named RAF Mount Batten) in 1918 where they served with Nos 237 and 238 Squadrons. Note the cylindrical air-bag, wing-tip floats.

N5750, one of Phoenix Dynamo's Maurice Farman Longhorns gets airborne from Royal Naval Air Station Redcar, Co. Durham in 1918.

Pupil-pilot and instructor prepare for a flight at RNAS Redcar in this Longhorn built by Phoenix Dynamo.

This drawing, which symbolised the production of the millionth shell at the Phoenix Works, was published in *Phoenix Bulletin* in 1918 to celebrate that total and the Armistice.

COW built about forty-five examples of the chunky Sopwith Snipe fighter during 1918. This one flew with the RAF's Central Flying School, No.23 Squadron and No.1 Flying Training School.

Eight 5.5in naval guns and mountings in the Coventry Ordnance Works factory in about 1918. COW built fifty-eight of these guns. These were among the 3,900 guns and howitzers of twenty-four different types it produced during the First World War.

Shortly before the War's end on 11 November 1918 COW was planning to mass-produce a $1\frac{1}{2}$ pounder automatic gun for use in aircraft. About a dozen types, including some one off designs, were equipped with this gun.

Part of the Phoenix Dynamo factory at Bradford with Felixstowe F.3 flying boats being built.

Forward hull sections of Felixstowe F.3s on articulated lorries at the Phoenix Dynamo factory. Because Royal Navy vehicles are being used the F.3s may be destined for Felixstowe.

This gathering of civil and Service personnel on Blackburn Aircraft Co.'s slip-way at Brough may indicate the launch and first flight of the first of Phoenix Dynamo's batch of thirty F.3s.

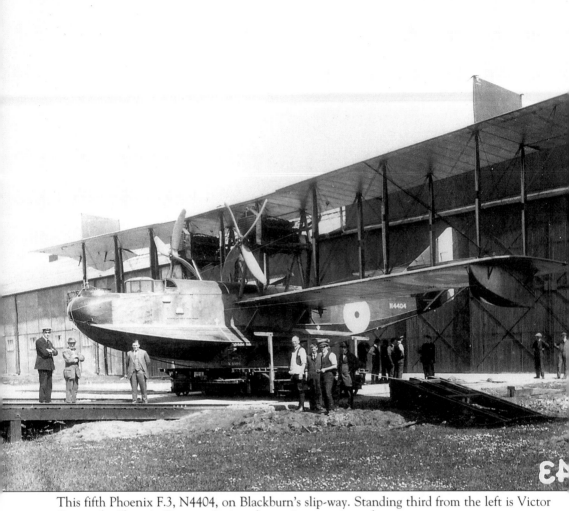

This fifth Phoenix F.3, N4404, on Blackburn's slip-way. Standing third from the left is Victor Gaunt, the Phoenix Company's aircraft-erection superintendent.

COW produced 450 RE.8 reconnaissance/bombers. This one, C5108, is seen in squadron service in the Middle East.

Felixstowe F.3, N4320, built by United Electric Car Works in Preston, pictured off the Isle of Grain on 15 May 1918 for Marine Aircraft Experimental Establishment anti-submarine hydrophone trials.

'You go down and I'll go up'. The same Felixstowe F.3, N4230, co-operates with a Royal Navy submarine, C25, during the MAEE's May 1918 hydrophone trials.

Production of Felixstowe F.3s in the United Electric Car Works in 1918. Note the four scimitar-bladed propellers and the under-wing bomb.

A Dick, Kerr Felixstowe F.3 on over-water patrol. Note the limp windsock on top of the upper wing and the two gunners in the nose position.

A well wrapped-up aircrew-man with his gaudily-painted Dick, Kerr Felixstowe F.3 at Felixstowe. The shape of the 'handed' propeller blades reveals that the 345hp Rolls-Royce Eagle engines turn them in opposite directions.

A Felixstowe F.5 at Felixstowe. Phoenix Dynamo built forty-five of these big flying boats.

Three

The Clipped Wings
of Victory

The end of the First World War on 11 November 1918 heralded swingeing cuts in aircraft orders and production programmes. Companies, which had beavered away for four wearying years churning out weapons of war, were forced to shrink their workforce and production facilities to peacetime levels. Phoenix Dynamo was one of them, shedding workers and its aircraft interests. However, Dick, Kerr's lively management viewed this situation as a challenge. Seeing an expanding market for tramcar and railway equipment, which had been neglected in wartime, it occupied part of the COW factory to produce them, leading to thoughts of amalgamations which, in December 1918, came to fruition with the formation of The English Electric Company Ltd (EECL). This company then bought out Phoenix Dynamo and COW and acquired a majority shareholding in Dick, Kerr whose associated companies Willans & Robinson and United Electric Car Co joined up too. Thus English Electric's five 'foundationer' companies had finally coalesced into a powerful industrial unit mainly producing their traditional products. But aeroplanes were not entirely forgotten; indeed Manning, now chief designer of EECL, produced projects for many different roles.

While the formation of EECL temporarily slowed the corporate interest in aviation, Manning was not deterred. Building the Fairey *Atalanta*, the Felixstowe F.3s, F.5s and the Corks had kick-started Manning's interest in this class of aeroplane. Among his projects was the M.1 biplane flying boat intended to meet a 1921 requirement for a Fleet spotter aircraft which could double as a trainer. This materialised as the M.3 Ayr. Its unique feature, which replaced drag-producing under-wing floats, was the use of short-span lower wings with marked dihedral to act as sponsons – or stabilisers – in the water. It was rumoured that bombs could be carried in the wing/sponsons. Underwater bomb bays? Highly unlikely! After launching, in March 1925, Marcus Manton, the Company's pilot, attempted to taxi the Ayr but it heeled over to one side. When the lower wing roots were immersed in water during an attempted take-off they caused too much drag and turbulence and the Ayr wouldn't get airborne. Extended trials didn't solve this problem and the Ayr was abandoned.

Another of Manning's projects resulted indirectly from the war's end Peace Treaty that prohibited Germany from importing or manufacturing military aeroplanes. To stimulate design work and maintain flying skills Germany took gliding to its bosom with clubs and competitions being organised nation-wide. This did not go entirely unnoticed in Britain, except by the Government. Aviation magazines regularly encouraged the sport of gliding. However, when the *Daily Mail* offered £1,000 as the prize for the longest duration flight in England completed by a glider of any nationality, things began to hum. The Royal Aero Club chose Itford in the Sussex Downs as the venue for the October 1922 competition. There were 35 entrants, the winner being the Frenchman Maneyrol in a Peyret tandem-winged monoplane.

Among the spectators was Manning, who immediately recognised the limitations of flight in gliders. He decided to design the simplest and lowest-powered aeroplane capable of lifting a man. This materialised as the S.1, a diminutive single-seat cantilever monoplane powered with an ABC motorcycle engine producing about 3hp but which, if thrashed to maximum revolutions, would deliver 7hp! The S.1 weighed only 250lb empty. Unusually for such a lightweight aeroplane, it was built under Air Ministry contract and named after Britain's smallest bird - the Wren.

The first Wren I, carrying the military serial J6973, was built in EECL's Dick, Kerr factory in Preston and was first flown by Squadron Leader Maurice Wright on 8 April 1923 at Lytham. It was then taken on Air Ministry charge and, with the New Types number 11, appeared in the RAF Pageant at Hendon. *Flight* magazine reported 'The Wren floated into the air like thistledown after help by a man at each wingtip to overcome the resistance of the tufty grass'. It was test flown at the Aeroplane Experimental Establishment (AEE), Martlesham Heath, before going to the Royal Aircraft Establishment (RAE) at Farnborough for strength testing. It was written off Air Ministry charge in June 1924.

Two more Wrens were built for the Motor-Glider Competition at Lympne in Kent where, numbered three and four, they achieved amazing distances for 'miles flown per gallon of fuel used'. Flight Lt Walter 'Scruffy' Longton (in the buff-coloured Wren 4) shared the prize for the longest flight on one gallon of petrol – 87.5 miles – with the Air Navigation and Engineering Co.'s ANEC 1 flown by Jimmy James.

The company offered new Wrens for sale at £350 but there were no takers. The Competition Wrens were stored, shown at Exhibitions – and neglected. Then, during 1956-1957, they were partially 'cannibalised' to make the 'new' Wren now with the Shuttleworth Trust.

Although the Cork flying boats were not ordered into production, Manning was encouraged to develop the second Cork prototype. With its 360hp Rolls-Royce Eagle VIII engines replaced by 450hp Napier Lion Ibs and modified airframe, it became the Cork III. This formed the basis for the design of a 1922 twin-engine flying boat, later named the Kingston, to meet Specification N23/23 for an anti-submarine and patrol aeroplane. The concept showed promise, so the Air Ministry ordered a prototype that was built in the Dick, Kerr factory. Its first flight in May 1924 at Lytham with Major Herbert Brackley as pilot, ended in disaster. It was believed that on take-off the aeroplane hit flotsam. This punched a hole in the hull which then filled with water tipping the Kingston onto its nose like a duck scrabbling for food on the bottom of a pond! It was beached, dismantled and repaired.

Despite this dramatic start to the Kingston programme, five pre-production Kingston Is, powered by 450hp Napier Lions turning two-bladed propellers were ordered and built during 1924-1926. When the first one was fitted with four-bladed propellers at the MAEE, now at Felixstowe, both Lions tore loose from their wing mountings as Flight Lieutenant David Carnegie got it airborne. The wings collapsed, cracking the hull. Apart from these take-off failures the Kingston exhibited a variety of snags. The Kingston II had a metal hull but retained the earlier wooden wings and other parts of the airframe.

The fifth and last aircraft became the Mk III, having a number of major differences from the earlier Kingstons. Its departure to Felixstowe in March 1926 marked the end of Kingston production, the Supermarine Southampton having been ordered 'off the drawing board' instead a year or so earlier. Without firm orders in sight, English Electric abandoned aircraft work and for the first time in his adult life W.O. Manning was without a full-time job. Instead, he became a consultant, participating in the design of Italy's little Fiat C.29 floatplane built for the 1927 Schneider Trophy Contest at Cowes. It did not, however, come to the start line.

Meanwhile the economic situation in Britain worsened with factory closures and wholesale unemployment becoming commonplace. EECL was badly affected and although the Preston factory had turned to building railway locomotives, other parts of the company were being sold off. By 1930 all Dick, Kerr's heavy engineering work had stopped and the factory was closed. In addition Coventry Ordnance Works had been sold.

A group of civil and Service personnel at Brough during August 1918 to watch the launch of
the pristine first prototype of the Phoenix Dynamo P.5 Cork anti-submarine patrol flying boat.

With two men aboard and three more hauling down on a rope attached to the tail, the two 360hp Rolls-Royce Eagle VIII engines of the Cork prototype, N86, are tested on the Brough slip-way.

The Cork prototype temporarily moored 'on the putty' in the River Humber at Brough. The two 'fins' on the top wing are pairs of fabric-enclosed king posts carrying bracing wires for the outboard wing sections.

N87, the Cork Mk II hangared at Brough in early 1919. It differed from the first aircraft, having its wings positioned on top of the hull, which was of slightly different design.

Final assembly by Dick, Kerr of the Fairey Atalanta I at Lytham. The Rolls-Royce Condor's installation is being checked using mock-ups of the push-me pull-you units. The small de Havilland DH6, G-EARL, belonged to H.B. Elwell of Lytham St Annes.

The completed Fairey Atalanta I on the slip-way of the MAEE, Isle of Grain in 1923 when it was the world's largest flying boat having a wingspan of 139ft.

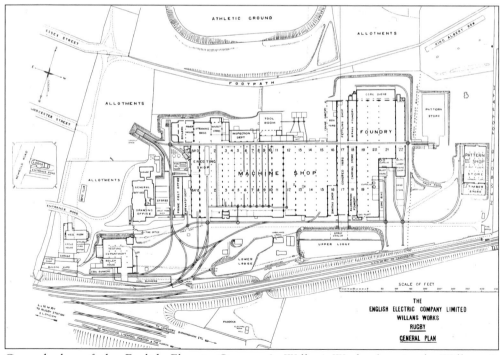

General plan of the English Electric Company's Willans Works (previously Willans & Robinson) at Rugby c.1920.

The Pattern Shop and Timber Stores at Willans Works advertises the locations of English Electric factories at Preston, Coventry, Bradford and Stafford.

In 1922 the Cork Mk II's Rolls-Royce engines were replaced by two 450hp Napier Lion engines. Designated Cork Mk III, it was one of several flying boats that toured UK flying-boat bases and the Scilly Isles.

Fuselage structure of English Electric's S1 ultra-light monoplane in Dick, Kerr's East Works, Strand Road, Preston in March 1923. Note Kingston hulls in the background and electric locomotives on the far right.

The Wren prototype, J6973, at the Aeroplane Experimental Establishment, Martlesham Heath, Suffolk, for handling trials as a trainer during August 1923. Earlier it flew in Hendon's RAF Pageant carrying the number eleven.

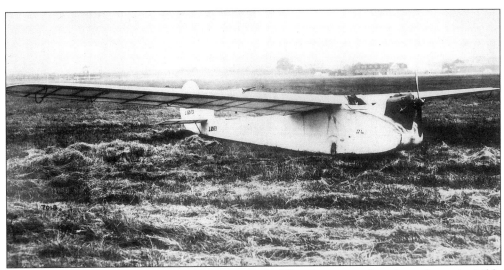

The pilot's head rests in a leading edge recess in the Wren's wing, making him almost invisible in this photograph of J6973 at Martlesham Heath. The tiny 7hp ABC engine perches on the Wren's nose.

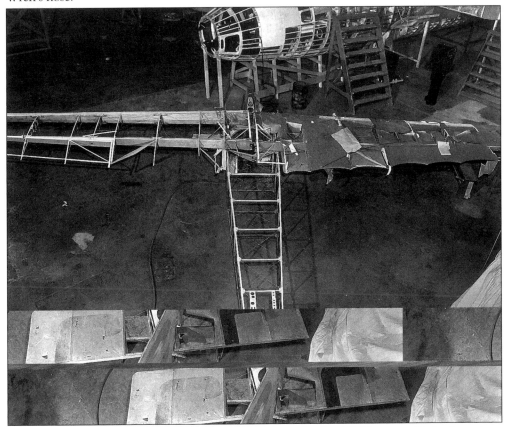

An irreparably damaged first Wren II, numbered three for the 1923 Lympne Light Aeroplane Trials, then civil registered G-EBNV in 1926. Parts of it helped the 1955 restoration of the third Wren to airworthy condition.

Second Wren II at Baginton Open Day in 1957. In that year it was handed into the care of the Shuttleworth Collection at Old Warden. In 1998, it was in an airworthy condition.

An excellent view of the Wren's tiny nose-mounted ABC engine with 3ft 6in diameter propeller. Who are with it? From left: F.W. Page, BAC Preston Division's chief engineer, Peter Hillwood, development test pilot, Bill Eaves and A.N. Other.

Peter Hillwood 'greases' the Wren back onto the runway after what is believed to be the first flight after the 1955 restoration.

The Kingston I's wooden hull being built. The multiple stringers and ribs were covered with layers of mahogany strips laid at an angle.

N168, the prototype Kingston coastal patrol and anti-submarine flying boat taxies before its disastrous take-off from the River Ribble on 22 May 1924. On the skyline are Lytham's St John's church spire and St Peter's tower.

N9710, a Kingston I, kicks up a flurry of water as it taxies quickly past some small craft moored off Lytham.

Lions *al fresco*. Close up of the Kingston I's Napier Lion engine installation. The cylindrical radiators and four-blade propellers are noteworthy.

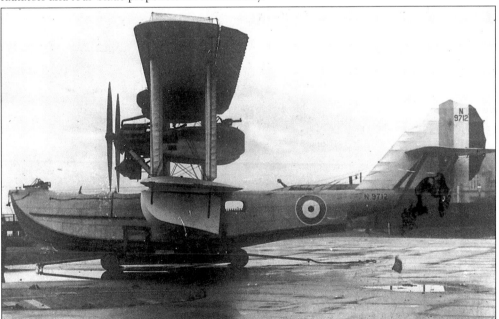

The metal-hulled Kingston II, had the same serial number as the last of the four Mk Is. The gunners' positions in the rear of the engine nacelles were described as 'noisy, hot, cold, smelly, dangerous, inaccessible in flight...'!

The Kingston II, N9712, taxies slowly in the Ribble off Lytham. The two 450hp Napier Lion engines were not cowled in the usual manner and this made their installation look somewhat unfinished.

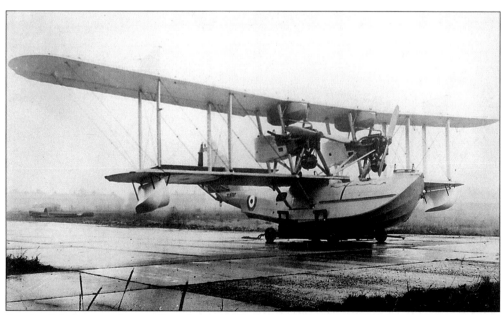

A splendid photograph revealing the major features of the Kingston II. The bulges under the upper wing are the 200 gallon tanks feeding fuel to the engines by gravity.

The English Electric Ayr. Two of these flying boats were ordered; only this one was built. The marked dihedral lower wings acted as sponsons to reduce the 'built-in head winds' of wingtip floats.

The parasol configuration of the Ayr's upper wing with the broad chord struts is clearly seen in this view.

Lots of detail in this view of the Ayr including the four-bladed propeller, small windscreen for the pilot, two open gunners' positions, cylindrical radiator below engine and other bits and bobs.

The heeled-over attitude of the Ayr when afloat was caused by the exaggerated dihedral angle of the lower wings/sponsons.

Four

War and Peace Again

It was against a highly uncertain economic background and with a sadly depleted aircraft industry that the Air Ministry, during the early 1930s launched a series of expansion plans for the RAF. As ever, the financing of these schemes plus the shortage of facilities to produce the hardware limited their success. By early 1938, after years of Britain's disarmament and appeasement policies, the strident re-occupation of the Rhineland by Nazi Germany, its massive rearmament programmes and general sabre-rattling activities plus the alarming growth of the Luftwaffe, began to loosen the Treasury's grip on the Defence purse strings. In April the Air Ministry's Scheme L called for the production of 12,000 new aircraft during the ensuing two years. There was no way that the established British aircraft manufacturers could produce this vast aerial fleet within that time scale. The Government's answer was to enlist the help of other engineering organisations with the required skills.

With its earlier experience English Electric was an immediate choice and, during the summer of 1938, was told that it was to build an initial batch of seventy-five Handley Page Hampden bombers. Appropriately, this aeroplane was named after John Hampden, the 17th Century defender of Civil Liberties. However, the Royal Air Force ignored that and because of its box-like front fuselage dubbed it 'the Flying Suitcase'! But where to build them? EECL soon began building extensions to its Preston factory. The next question was 'Where do we test the Hampdens?' The little Wrens had been flown from Lytham Sands, clearly unsuitable for a near nine ton twin-engine bomber. Eventually a site was selected at Samlesbury, about five miles from Blackburn. On top of all this planning and building, the Air Ministry also told EECL to get ready to produce the even bigger Handley Page Halifax, a four-engine monster which tipped the scales at over seventeen tons – and that was without any warload.

One feature of the company's development which was to have very long term benefits was the establishment in 1939 of a small design group. Its job in life was to look after some of the 1,200 modifications that were made to the Halifax during its operational career plus many others on the Hampden. But more of that later.

By the time the first Preston-built Hampden flew on 22 February 1940, the type was pioneering the RAF's sea-mining techniques in the Norwegian campaign. By the end of April EECL's production rate was five aircraft a month but this increased rapidly and 260 Hampdens were built by the year's end. When the last one left the factory in March 1942, EECL had produced 770 Hampden Is for the RAF, almost exactly half of the total 1,581 built. The many 'milestone' operations in which these EECL-built aircraft were involved include the first bombing attack on Berlin during the night of 25-6 August 1940 by five squadrons of Hampdens. Meanwhile, Halifax production had begun at Strand Road.

The first of these big bombers, which the RAF soon re-named 'the Hallybag', got airborne from Samlesbury on 15 August 1941, beginning a vast manufacturing and delivery programme. Production rate peaked in February 1944 when eighty-eight aircraft were delivered.

Apart from Handley Page, which build 1,590 Halifaxes, two other production 'conglomerates' were set up which jointly delivered 1,732 aircraft. EECL outstripped them by building a grand total of 2,145 Halifaxes. Among these was Halifax II, V9977, which was the first bomber to be fitted with the H2S radar navigational and bombing aid. Its first experimental flight was made from Hurn on 16 April 1942. Sadly it crashed some seven weeks later at Welsh Bicknor, Gloucestershire, with the loss of its crew and six scientists. Another Preston-built 'Hallybag' II, W1048, continues to make history. It was shot down over Norway during the night of 27-28 April 1942 during No.25 Squadron's attempt to bomb the German battleship *Tirpitz* in Trondheim Fjord. It crashed onto the frozen freshwater Lake Hoklingen and was abandoned by its crew, who became prisoners of war, sinking 90ft to the bottom. In 1973 it was raised by a British recovery team and returned to the UK. Fortunately, corrosion was minimal even after thirty-one years underwater. After restoration this Halifax is now in Hendon's RAF Bomber Command Museum, the sole surviving example of its type.

In addition to new aircraft deliveries, older ones returned to the factory for modifications, often without being checked before leaving the squadron. A gun on one aircraft still had 'one up the spout' – a round left in the breech. When it was being checked on arrival at Samlesbury, someone accidentally pulled the trigger resulting in a neat hole in the hangar doors. Another aircraft's flare tubes still had flares in them and some aircraft still had personal items left in by the aircrew.

Towards the end of 1942 EECL acquired yet another company. This was the comparatively small aero-engine manufacturer D. Napier & Son Ltd at Acton. With some 130 years experience in the engineering business but only twenty of them in aviation, before the Second World War began Napier's Major Frank B. Holford was converting a 1930s diesel aero-engine to petrol fuel to create the mighty 2,000hp liquid-cooled 24-cylinder flat-H Sabre. It was intended for the new Hawker Typhoon fighter of which 3,330 were to be built by the Gloster Aircraft Co. To meet the demand for the Sabre, a new factory controlled by EECL was built in Liverpool. However, production problems delayed Sabre deliveries and Typhoon entry to RAF squadrons. The author recalls fitting 'slave' engines to new Typhoon airframes so that they could be flown away from Gloster's factory to nearby RAF Aston Down airfield. Then they would be followed by road so as to remove the Sabre, take it back to the factory and refit it to yet another new airframe for a repeat performance.

But EECL's finest hours as an aircraft manufacturer were still some way off. When Halifax production was at its peak during early 1944 the Ministry of Aircraft Production was agonising over a successor on the Samlesbury and Strand Road production lines. Finally, in June 1944, as the Allied landings in Normandy were under way, instructions came for EECL to build de Havilland Vampire single-seat single-engine jet fighters. This was because de Havilland's factories were filled with Mosquitoes, Hornets, Sea Hornets and Doves. Undoubtedly EECL's fine record of Hampden and Halifax production paved the way for the Vampire contract. Just a month after that W.E.W. 'Teddy' Petter was appointed chief engineer of the EECL's Aircraft Division.

It is said that the flap of a butterfly's wing in a Brazilian jungle begins a movement of air that grows into a Force 10 storm in Florida. Be that as it may, the circumstances which took Petter from Yeovil to Preston began ten years earlier in Westland Aircraft Co.'s boardroom. When 'Teddy', son of company chairman Sir Ernest Petter, one of the twin brothers who founded Westland, was co-opted to the Board and ranked equal with the long-serving general manager, the managing director Robert Bruce decided that nepotism had gone too far. He resigned. Then, Geoffrey Hill, who had conceived the unique family of Westland's tail-less Pterodactyl monoplanes, learned that the 'infant prodigy' was soon to be appointed technical director at the tender age of thirty-five. He too packed his bags.

But young Petter was nobody's fool. While at Westland he designed the Lysander army co-operation aircraft of which some 1,650 were built as well as the eye-catching Whirlwind twin-engine fighter which had too many design novelties for its own good – including having engine exhaust pipes routed through the fuel tanks – and which equipped only two RAF squadrons. Then he designed the slender-winged twin-engine Welkin high altitude fighter that never entered RAF service. Finally, he was responsible for the initial concept of the big Wyvern naval strike aircraft of which 124 were built, some serving in the October 1956 Suez Campaign. In 1944 he was working on the design of a twin-jet fighter-bomber following some encouragement by the Ministry of Aircraft Production and interest by the Air Ministry. Every one of these Petter designs was unorthodox, reflecting the eccentric but innovative side of his nature.

For much of the decade of his role as technical director, Petter hankered after the role of Westland's chief engineer, but was described as 'intolerant of his colleagues, demanding for himself absolute control of the company in all its aspects' and as 'difficult, brilliant, eccentric, intense and dictatorial'. However, the almost equally young vice-chairman, Eric Mensforth and the Minister of Aircraft Production, Sir Stafford Cripps, would not agree with Petter's demands. So Petter shook the dust of Yeovil off his feet and set out for Preston to join EECL and head up the small design team there. He did not go empty-handed. With Mensforth's agreement, Petter took with him his preliminary designs and proposals for the twin-jet fighter-bomber.

The official caption to this photograph reads 'Line of Hampdens at Samlesbury'. The rear fuselage minus its tail unit in the lower left corner belongs to Hampden P1202, built by Handley Page, which was being repaired.

Strand Road, Preston, November 1941. Front fuselages of seventeen of the 770 Handley Page Hampden I twin-engine bombers built by English Electric.

Shortly before the previous picture was taken the Luftwaffe had photographed Preston's docks and English Electric's Strand Road factory, which is described as being 'for electrical machinery'. Neither docks nor factory were bombed during the war.

An English Electric-built Hampden I of No.455 Squadron RAAF photographed during May 1942. That month No.455, based at RAF Leuchars, was transferred from Bomber to Coastal Command for torpedo bombing.

Its port outer engine partly uncowled, Halifax II Series I (Special), JB928, outside Samlesbury's No.4 Shed. Note turret-less nose and early 'Hallybag Handbag' fins and rudders. It was lost attacking Gelsenkirchen with No.78 Squadron on 26 June 1943. 'Hallybag' was RAF-speak for 'Halifax'.

The need for so many overhead hoists in Samlesbury's No.2 Shed during July 1944 is self evident in this photograph of the 'marry-up' stage of Halifax Mk III production. Note the amount of equipment already installed.

Vampire front fuselage assembly in 171 Shop, K Block, Strand Road during 1945. Note the third fuselage in a 'turn-over' fixture.

Pairs of port and starboard Vampire wings being assembled. Let's hope that the box of drills in the air intake of the nearest wing was removed before delivery!

John D. Rose (right), English Electric's chief test pilot, flew Hampdens and Halifaxes and finally Vampires. He was not impressed with the latter type. On the left is George Gilbraith, a Company flight engineer who flew with him.

TG278, the fifth of the first batch of de Havilland Goblin-powered Vampire F1 jet fighters built by English Electric. Its twin boom configuration contributed to the first choice of the name Spider Crab. This was soon changed to Vampire

TG278 was later used for trials of the de Havilland Ghost engine. With wingspan increased by eight feet, John Cunningham, de Havilland's chief test pilot set a world height record of 59,446ft on 23 March 1948.

The pilot of this Vampire I eyeballs the camera as he positions his aircraft for a close-up view. Cockpit, nose landing gear, armament and engine were all packed into the egg-shaped fuselage.

Extra 'Elephant ear' air intakes fed the double-sided impeller of the Rolls-Royce Nene engine experimentally-fitted in TX807, the third Vampire II. In Australia it aided Nene-powered Vampire Mk30 development.

A Vampire III carries pylon-mounted, long-range 100 gallon under-wing fuel tanks. As they adversely affected longitudinal stability the entire tail unit was redesigned and became standardised on Vampires.

John Squier, English Electric's chief production test pilot, was fortunate to escape with his life on 3 November 1947 after this Canadian Vampire III engine stopped providing its usual surge on take-off.

The first of eighteen Sea Vampire 20 fighters, VV136 first got airborne in October 1948. It had strengthened, clipped wings, modified landing gear and an arrester hook hinged above the jet pipe.

Five

The Jet Generation

Between 1944 and 1952 some 1,370 Vampires of six different Marks were built. This great sub-contract production programme enabled EECL to stay in business as an aircraft manufacturer when it had no designs of its own to build. It gained the company wide experience of jet aircraft production and test-flying, established its credentials as a major aircraft manufacturer and provided work for hundreds of its employees at a time when, in the post-war years, the aircraft industry had shrunk in size. De Havilland took three standard Vampire fuselages from the Strand Road production line and with them built three DH 108 high-speed research aircraft, the third of which, on 9 September 1948, became the first aeroplane to fly faster than sound in Britain. Admittedly, it was going down hill at the time, but this was no mean achievement for an aircraft built partly of wood! For about three years, beginning at the end of 1945, Samlesbury also modified some 200 Avro Lincoln bombers. These bigger brothers of the renowned Lancaster passed through the EECL 'sausage machine' where updated 'electrickery' and equipment were installed.

Soon after Petter's arrival in Preston, while he was still working on the jet fighter-bomber proposals, the Air Ministry had one of its 'changes of direction' and issued a new requirement indicating that what it really, really wanted was a high altitude jet bomber instead. It was back to the drawing board for the designers. By the autumn of 1945, the aircraft's design had changed. Designated the English Electric A1, it was offered to the Air Ministry which, in January 1946, ordered four prototypes. At a stroke – as they say – Petter's design facilities and those at Samlesbury were too limited for the testing and development of this new aeroplane.

The solution lay only a few miles away. On the bank of the River Ribble estuary at Warton was a large, virtually unused RAF airfield which, during 1942-1945 had been used by the US Army Air Force as a base for the repair and overhaul of some 10,000 US-built aircraft and 6,000 aero-engines. English Electric refurbished the buildings and installed new research and development equipment. It also appointed a new chief test pilot; Wing Commander Roland Beamont, a gallant RAF pilot with substantial test flying experience in the Service and with the Gloster and de Havilland companies. Perhaps of more importance, English Electric undertook studies of supersonic flight. More of that later on. Keep reading.

It was from Warton that the shiny sky-blue English Electric A1 bomber, powered by Rolls-Royce Avon engines, made its first flight on Friday 13 May 1949 piloted by Beamont. He was accompanied on the 30 minute flight by chief production test pilot John Squier acting as 'minder' in a Vampire chase aircraft. Shortly afterwards the A1 was given the type name Canberra and the four prototypes were designated B1s. The Royal Australian Air Force had shown an interest in this aircraft even before its first flight. What better way to start turning that interest into orders than by naming the new bomber after Australia's capital city?

Just four months after the A1's first flight, Beamont took it to the Society of British Aircraft Constructors' (SBAC) Exhibition and Display at Farnborough. But there were problems only seconds before the Canberra became airborne for its display.

Due to a misunderstanding about minimum amounts of fuel required in the fuel tanks for the system to work properly, at the very moment that Beamont was lining up for take-off the port engine stopped and smoke billowed from the jet pipe. Some quick juggling of the programme moved the Canberra to the final display slot. This time Beamont's highly aerobatic display stole the show. The high speed runs, rolls and half loops astounded everyone. On the Saturday Display there was another white-knuckle moment for most of the 150,000 spectators. As Beamont approached the runway with landing gear down and bomb bay doors open after his five-minute slot, several black objects were seen to fall from the aircraft. From the Control Tower came the call 'Canberra – you're dropping pieces!' Beamont then discovered that all instruments for the starboard engine indicated 'zero'. Fortunately *his* knuckles were still the correct colour. As the engine was still running perfectly he made a faultless landing as the Control Tower added 'Canberra, you're trailing wires and things from the fuselage!' Back in the hangar it was found that the breeze had plucked some auto-observer equipment from the open bomb bay, breaking electrical connections to the engine.

The Canberra soon attracted world-wide attention, particularly in the United States. In the late summer of 1950 the aircraft was demonstrated to senior US Air Force officials in the UK and USA with talk of licensed production 'across the pond'. This turned to fact in July 1953 when the first US-built Canberra, designated the B-57, flew. It led some 400 more B-57s, licence-produced by Martin Aircraft in six different variants, into US skies. Australia's Government Aircraft Factory flew the first of forty-eight licence-built Canberras in May 1953, delivering the last one to the RAAF some five years later.

In Britain Canberras for the RAF and for export initially were turned out by EECL factories. As the Canberra order book threatened to swamp these production facilities, sub-contract production began in the Handley Page factories at Radlettt and Cricklewood, by Shorts in Belfast (which developed and flew the U.10 and U.14 unmanned target Canberras), and at A.V. Roe's Woodford facility at Manchester. An interesting 1957 Handley Page project was the HP113, a twin-jet 8-12 seat executive aeroplane using a Canberra front fuselage. It never left the pages of its brochure. Boulton Paul Aircraft became prime contractor for development and testing of some Canberra variants and modifications.

No.101 Squadron, at RAF Binbrook, Lincolnshire, was the first to re-equip with dedicated jet bombers when a trio of Canberra B2s arrived in January 1951. It was another four months before No.101 got all its Canberras. But this was just the start. Some fifty-five RAF Squadrons and training units and several Royal Navy units flew Canberras of bewildering variety. The T4 trainer, the camera-laden photo-reconnaissance PR3 and PR9, the B6 bomber and B(I)8 night intruder; then came the B15 and B16 strike variants able to operate as ground attack aircraft or in the tactical nuclear or conventional 'iron-bombing' roles, the T11, T19 and E15 radar trainers and calibration aircraft, the unique 'wart-nosed' T17 electronic counter measures trainer to simulate jamming signals from Warsaw Pact aircraft, and the TT18 target towers.

The Canberra was a major export money-spinner, large numbers of new and ex-RAF aircraft being sold to sixteen overseas countries. Canberras were used 'in anger' by the RAF in Malaya from 1955 and in the Suez Campaign of 1956. A little-known conflict involving Canberras was in the Congo in 1961 when the Indian Air Force was part of a six-nation UN force formed to bring the breakaway province of Katanga back under the control of the new Congo Central Government. B-57s were used by the United States Air Force in Vietnam beginning in 1965. During the 1965 war between India and Pakistan the Indian Air Force flew Canberras while the Pakistan Air Force operated B-57s! The *Fuerza Aerea Argentina* flew Canberras against British land forces and Royal Navy ships during the 1982 Falklands Campaign,

It is recorded that a total of 1,376 Canberras were built. Quantity aside, there is no doubting the quality and effectiveness of the Canberra, which was an outstanding aeroplane in very many ways. As Bob Hotz, one-time Editor of the US aerospace magazine *Aviation Week & Space Technology*, wrote 'The performance of the Canberra in all its variants over more than two decades has assured it of a well-carved niche in the galaxy of great combat aircraft'. In October 1998 five Canberra PR9s and four T4s were still flying with No.39(1 PRU) Squadron at RAF Marham. Their main task is survey and mapping but they have flown high altitude reconnaissance sorties over Bosnia, Yugoslavia and Zaire. They are expected to serve until 2003.

With the Canberra design launched, Edward Petter's mind was full of supersonics, his thoughts being channelled in that direction by a Ministry of Supply initiative aimed at getting Britain's aircraft industry geared up to build supersonic aircraft. His design proposal went to the Ministry in 1948 and some eighteen months of hard work produced all the basic design features. By this time the aeroplane had been designated the P.1. Then Petter suddenly changed horses in mid-stream. Having launched the design of the P.1, which would be developed into a heavy, complex and expensive single-seat fighter, he suddenly went all 'lightweight and simple'. He resigned from English Electric early in 1950 and joined Folland Aircraft as deputy managing director where, the following year, he succeeded Harry Folland as managing and technical director and created designs for the diminutive Midge and then the Gnat lightweight fighter. At last he was top of the complete heap, the role he had always coveted. He was succeeded at EECL by thirty-four year old Frederick William Page who became chief engineer. Freddy Page had joined the Company in 1945 after some seven years with Hawker Aircraft Ltd. He was to shoulder the burden of responsibility for P.1 design and its development into the Lightning. Just a few weeks later in April 1950, EECL was given an order to build three P.1 prototypes.

To obtain 'hands on' experience of low-speed flying in an aeroplane with the design configuration chosen, Shorts built the SB.5. It had the unique ability to fly with three different angles of wing sweep and the tail-plane in two different positions. It was first flown by Shorts' chief test pilot Tom Brooke-Smith at the Aeroplane and Armament Experimental Establishment (A&AEE), Boscombe Down on 2 December 1952 with 50° of wing sweep and a fin-top tail-plane. Later this was increased to 60° with a fuselage-mounted tail-plane.

Work on the P.1A prototypes progressed rapidly and Beamont flew the first one on 4 August 1954 at A&AEE. Seven days later it created history, becoming Britain's first aircraft to exceed Mach 1.0 in level flight. The next step towards an operational supersonic fighter was taken with three P.1B prototypes. On 25 November 1958 a P.1B became the first British aircraft to reach Mach 2.0.

Learning from past experience with the Gloster Javelin, where the ordering of too few aircraft for a complex development programme had delayed its entry into RAF squadrons, a further twenty P.1B development aircraft had been ordered in February 1954. It was to be five-and-a-half years before the first production Lightning F1 flew in October 1959. Two months later Lightnings entered RAF service with the Central Fighter Establishment's Air Fighting Development Squadron. On 29 June 1960 No.74 Squadron, whose motto is '*I Fear No Man*', received its first Lightnings.

Inevitably, during the Lightning's development programme, there were many problems to be solved – like the loss of cockpit canopies at high and supersonic speed. A much more alarming incident occurred on 1 October 1959 when John Squier experienced total loss of control in the prototype Lightning T4 two-seat trainer. This was over the Solway Firth at 40,000ft and near twice the speed of sound! In this horrifying situation the ejection system worked perfectly, his parachute opened automatically, and dropped him into water. The fact that he was the first man to survive a 1,200 mph ejection was certainly the last thing on his mind as he floated in his inflatable dinghy, hoping that his emergency radio beacon would pinpoint his location. It didn't. An air-sea search was abandoned at nightfall and it was feared he had not survived. Then, some thirty hours later he managed to paddle to the shore at Gorleston in Wigton Bay and stagger to a local school, from where he was taken to hospital. After a few weeks rest he was back flying again.

Meanwhile, EECL was again looking to the future. At the same time the Ministry of Supply was formulating a requirement, known as GOR 339, for a Canberra replacement. When it was issued the Ministry stressed that an order would go only to a partnership of manufacturers. There followed a long and tortuous series of events within Britain's aircraft industry, Government corridors of power and the Royal Air Force. Suffice it to say that in December 1958, English Electric and Vickers-Armstrong (Aircraft) were named as partners to produce this new aeroplane, the TSR.2. In order to amalgamate their aviation interests, English Electric's Aircraft Division became a separate entity named English Electric Aviation Ltd (EEAL).

While Vickers-Armstrong was nominated prime contractor, all work was divided between the two partners. EEAL was to design and manufacture the wings, rear fuselage and tail unit plus their systems and equipment. Vickers had similar responsibility for the rest of the aircraft.

As this work began, EEAL underwent another phased reorganisation. Following the British Government's policy of rationalisation of the aircraft industry through the formation of larger groupings of companies, in 1960 Bristol Aeroplane Company, English Electric and the Vickers Group revealed their intention to pool their aviation interests in a new holding company. Named the British Aircraft Corporation (BAC) it had three subsidiary companies: Bristol Aircraft Ltd, English Electric Aviation Ltd and Vickers-Armstrongs (Aircraft) Ltd. Luton based Hunting Aircraft Ltd became another subsidiary.

While this re-alignment of companies was underway, development of what was now known as the BAC Lightning continued apace with no less than seven variants being produced. But the 're-organisers' of this world had not yet finished with EEAL. In January 1964, along with the other two BAC subsidiaries, it became a BAC Division losing its spirited 'English Electric' name to become the soul-less 'British Aircraft Corporation (Operating) Ltd - Preston Division'. Even this was to be only a temporary name!

Lightning production reached the modest total of only 340 aircraft built principally for the RAF. They equipped nine front-line squadrons, and six other units. From its peak years of 1968-70, when some 150 Lightnings were in RAF squadron service, the progressive run-down of the Lightning force continued until 1977 when about thirty-five remained in service – although Lightning production had virtually ended some six years earlier. Export orders for Lightnings were disappointingly small. In 1966 Saudi Arabia had ordered a mixed bag of forty-nine single and two seat Lightnings and, in the same year, Kuwait placed an order for fourteen Lightnings. They helped production to continue for about three years.

A really classy chassis. Roly Beamont banks the A.1 showing the clean overall appearance of this beautiful shiny all-blue aeroplane. The lumps and bumps would be added later!

This photograph, dated 8 May 1949, shows the A.1 prototype, VN799, just having been towed from its Warton hangar. Its first flight came five days later. Note the rounded top rudder and the dorsal fin.

While part of Strand Road's factories produced aircraft in 1953, West Works' Rolling Stock Erection Department built locomotives for Rhodesia and Gold Coast Railways. Ducts from the second loco on the left indicate engine-running checks. At the rear is the prototype Deltic locomotive.

This head-on view of the A.1 prototype emphasises the smooth streamlined shape of the fuselage and engine nacelles and the stark straight lines of the wing and tail unit.

Members of Warton's Design Office Equipment Group in 1950. Standing from left: Harry Daykin, Ralph Parker, Ian Webster, Stan Powderhill, Jack Wilcock, Bill Brown. Seated from left: Clarence Cowburn, -?-, George Turner. Sadly, their leader, Charlie Humphries was absent.

First flown on 9 November 1949, VN813, the second Canberra B1 prototype's engine nacelles swallow the Rolls-Royce Nene centrifugal flow turbo-jets with ease. This aeroplane was flown by Rolls-Royce during Nene development.

Prototypes on parade! From the front are Canberra B1s VN799 with its name on the nose; VN828 with no dorsal fin; VN813; VN850 early in 1950. Note Warton's ex-USAAF lattice-type air traffic control tower.

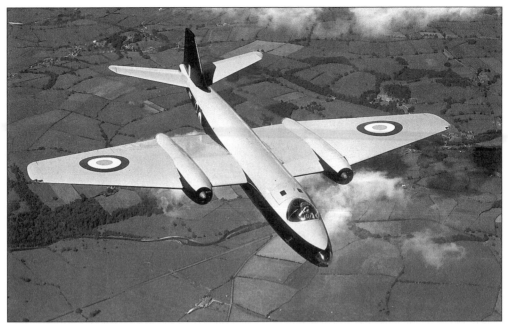

The pilot of VX165, the first Canberra B2 prototype, salutes the cameraman in the photographic aircraft. This was the first Canberra to have a glazed nose for the bomb-aimer.

Working lunch for Canberra design team members. From left to right: W.E.W. Petter (chief engineer), H.C. Harrison (production designer), E.J. Nichol (chief designer – Dowty Equipment Ltd), F.D. Crowe (chief draughtsman).

Airborne by Avro. The first Canberra B2, WJ971, to be built by A.V. Roe first flew at the company's Woodford airfield on 25 November 1952. A.V. Roe built 100 Canberra B2s.

Canberra B2, WJ716, arrives at the RAE Farnborough to appear in the 1953 SBAC Flying Display. This aircraft subsequently flew with No.9 Squadron, then based at RAF Binbrook, Lincolnshire.

The first Glenn L. Martin RB-57A produced in 1953 at the US company's Middle River, Baltimore, Maryland plant.

US Martin B-57Bs on the ramp at the Middle River plant. This variant was the basis for a number of others for widely differing operational roles for US Air Force.

A Martin RB-57D reconnaissance aircraft converted to an EB-57D for use as a Defence Systems Evaluation aircraft. Note the 106ft span wing, restyled nacelles and nose.

With maulstick and brush poised the sign-writer records in August 1955 yet another World Altitude Record of 65,876ft on the nose of the Olympus-powered Canberra 2.

'This round's on me'! Canberra B2, WH734 was used for flight refuelling trials during 1959. Here, acting as the tanker, it makes a 'dry hook-up' – no fuel involved – with the fifty-seventh production Gloster Javelin, XH780, carrying two 'bosom tanks'.

A Canberra cockpit. It looks more like a Second World War bomber than a jet aircraft but the design of instruments and cockpit equipment had not kept pace with that of the airframe and engines.

Canberra B2, WK161, with infrared suppression jet pipes, was used for 'Stealth' technology development by the RAE at Farnborough during the early 1970s. Boulton Paul Aircraft applied special DX3 radar-absorbing material to the aircraft.

On 26 August 1952 VX185, prototype Canberra B5, became the first aircraft to cross the Atlantic twice in one day. Including a two-hour turn-around in Gander, Newfoundland, its 'double dash' took 10hours and 3minutes. Pilots were Beamont and Hillwood with Watson as navigator.

Five Canberras were entered in the Speed Section of the England – New Zealand Air Race in 1953. The winner was a Canberra PR3, WE139, which averaged 494.5mph over the 11,800 mile flight. This aircraft, numbered three, is seen with other entrants at London Heathrow Airport before the start on 8 October 1953.

A photograph, dated 28 April 1954, showing five basic Canberra marks. From front; WH797 camera-carrying PR7; WJ755 B6 bomber; WH846 T4 trainer; WE135 PR3; WH715 B2. The B(I)8 interdictor aircraft and the PR9 appeared later.

Boulton Paul Aircraft designed and built this 'flash-pack' seen on the wingtip of a photographic reconnaissance Canberra PR3.

A Canberra B(I)6 reveals all as it banks for the cameraman. It carries two 1,000lb bombs on under-wing pylons and a battery of four 20mm Hispano cannon in a belly pack.

D. Napier & Son Ltd used WK163, a Canberra B2, to test fly its Double Scorpion rocket motor seen under the fuselage beneath the wing trailing edge. Flown by Napier's Mike Randrup it set a new World Altitude Record of 70,308ft on 28 August 1957. During the summer of 1998 it appeared in a number of UK air-shows, operated by Classic Aviation Projects.

This Canberra B6 built by Short Brothers was part of a batch converted to B15s at Samlesbury. The trial installation of the French Nord AS.30 air-to-surface missile seen here was carried out by Boulton Paul Aircraft.

A Canberra PR7 photographic reconnaissance aircraft. This variant as well as Canberra PR3s and PR9s equipped eleven RAF Squadrons, serving from December 1952 until May 1982.

An impressive line of Canberra wings and fuselages at Warton being refurbished to extend their operational life.

The fourth production Canberra B(I)8 interdictor aircraft designed for the night intruder role with 2nd Tactical Air Force based in Germany. It carries its four-cannon main armament in a belly pack.

Note the fighter-type cockpit canopy offset to port on this interdictor Canberra. This one carries two 240 gallon wing-tip tanks and two bombs.

This belly pack containing four 20mm cannon was designed and built by Boulton Paul Aircraft for the interdictor Canberras.

XH130, the second production Canberra PR9 gets airborne at Sydenham, Belfast where a batch of these aircraft with increased wingspan and updated equipment were produced by Short Brothers.

The hinged nose of this Canberra PR9 enabled the navigator to gain access to his ejection seat. When No.39 Squadron RAF disbanded on 29 May 1982, its Canberras were the last with an operational squadron.

Shorts designated this Canberra their SC9. In fact it was a PR9, XH132, converted in 1960 by Shorts to carry an infra-red installation in a restyled nose for trials of the Red Top missile.

Converted from a Canberra B2, this U10 unmanned target aircraft takes off from Shorts' Sydenham airfield in the hands of a human pilot.

As Oliver Cromwell said 'Show me – warts and all'. This Canberra T17 electronic counter measures trainer's 'warts' hid electronic 'kit' to simulate Warsaw Pact airborne jamming devices during NATO exercises.

Close-up of a Canberra B2 during conversion to a T17 at Boulton Paul Aircraft. The side-mounted transmitting 'device' lacks its covering and the angled bulkhead awaits a fairing.

A Canberra T17 of No.360 Squadron when based at RAF Cottesmore in 1973. Note the number of blisters, cooling air intakes, and strakes plus the serial number on its underside.

Once a Canberra B2, now it's a TT18 target-towing aircraft. Modified by Flight Refuelling Ltd, its under-wing pod carries a winch driven by a Dowty ram air turbine. The target is streamed on a 10mile long cable.

During the early 1970s, seven Canberra PR7s were converted to T22s for Buccaneer navigator training and radar calibration duties. Their long pointed noses covering Blue Parrot radar were a dead give-away to identifying these aircraft.

One of a number of Canberra B(I)56s built for the *Fuerza Aerea del Peru*. Note that it carries the British Class B registration G27-99 allocated to English Electric, plus its own aircraft serial number.

A Venezuelan Canberra B(I)88 at Warton ready for delivery to the *Fuerzas Aereas Venezolanas*.

This Canberra B62 built for the *Fuerza Aerea Argentina* carried British civil registration G-AYHP when it flew in the SBAC Display at Farnborough in September 1970.

Some 280 employees who had been associated with the Canberra turned out at Samlesbury on 13 May 1969 to mark the twentieth Anniversary of its first flight. Here are most of them with Canberra B2, WH719, which was refurbished for export to Peru later that year.

RAF Wyton, 13 May 1989. Forty Canberras of eight different Marks gathered for the fortieth Anniversary of the type's first flight. A T4 trainer, WT478, painted to represent the all-blue prototype, flew with Roly Beamont in the second seat this time!

The Short SB5 research aircraft built to flight test several configurations for the English Electric P.1. Its wings could be attached at three different sweep angles and the tail-plane in two places. Here it flies with 60° sweep and fin top tail-plane.

ENGLISH ELEC. NEG. AWS/8/852 C (ACKNOWLEDGE)

The all-metal finished P.1A prototype, WG760, at Boscombe Down in July 1954. The 'double-decked' installation of the two 8,500lb thrust Armstrong Siddeley Sapphire engines and their egg-shaped air intake are noteworthy.

English Electric had already decided that the low tail-plane position was correct for the P.1 when the SB5 first flew with this configuration in October 1953. Note the drooped inboard leading edges of the wings.

Their top speeds were about 1,500mph apart, but they were both single-seat monoplanes and both flying at Warton in July 1957. The Wren is airborne while Roly Beamont takes a firm grip of the P.1A's access ladder.

The prototype P.1B, XA847, first flew on 4 April 1957 and was used for trials of the reheat system.

A bow-wave of chippings is produced during gravel-arrested landing trials with P.1B XA847 at RAE Farnborough during 1966-67. As the P.1F with the extended fin it carries here, it was earlier flown on aerodynamic trials.

The second prototype P.1B first flew on 5 September 1957. (Incidentally, someone suggested that this new fighter should be named the Pib!) Here it carries a brace of dummy de Havilland Firestreak missiles.

The fourth of 20 pre-production Lightnings ordered, XG310, seen at Boulton Paul Aircraft's Seighford, Staffs airfield where, in 1962, that company was involved in the Lightning F.3 development programme.

'Ah - that's better'. XG310, now converted to the Lightning F3 aerodynamic prototype, has the latest square-tipped fin and carries a ventral fuel tank.

Clearly, it was fun working in Warton's Flying Controls Group in October 1959. Back row from left: Martin Walsh, Morris Jones, Bob Rigg, Harry Bonney, Don Bradley, George Miles, Bob Sharples, Reg Parker, Nev Johnson. Front row: John Riley, Fred Wills, Bill Parker, Law Nichols, Jack Wilcock, Dennis Liddle, Larry Abram.

English Electric test pilots. From left are Desmond de Villiers, Peter Hillwood, Jimmy Dell, Don Knight, with Roland Beamont on the ladder.

No.74 Squadron was the first to get Lightning F1s. Here they show the 'tiger's teeth' fuselage markings. Jimmy Dell delivered the first one, on 29 June 1960.

Firestreak-armed Lightning F1s, of No.74 Squadron, fly a tight, nine-ship, arrow formation.

The men working on this Lightning fuselage emphasise its size. Its two Rolls-Royce Avon engines fitted neatly, one above the other, in the rear section.

This Lightning F1A first flew on 20 September 1960. It had a busy life with A&AEE followed by English Electric at Warton, then No.56 Squadron and finally No.226 OCU before being scrapped in July 1974.

A Lightning F1A, XM177, seconds before touch down, Note the lowered flaps and position of the tail plane. Originally flown by No.56 Squadron, here it appears to have the yellow-black-yellow nose markings of RAF Wattisham Target Facilities Flight plus No.11 Squadron fin-markings.

The first Lightning F2, XN723. It was virtually identical to the F1 but had an updated cockpit and some equipment and systems improvements.

'Scramble!' When the klaxon sounded in the Battle Flight at RAF Gutersloh, West Germany, everyone ran – pilots and ground crew alike. Here No.19 Squadron personnel race to get their Lightning F2A into the air. ASAP!

Built as the first Lightning F3, XP693 flew on 16 June 1962 but was converted to F3A (Interim F6) standard around January 1967. Note the square fin-tip, over-wing tanks, flight refuelling probe and Red Top missile.

A Lightning F3 of No.74 Squadron up in the sunshine sometime in the mid-1960s. It later served with Nos 56 and 29 Squadrons. Note Firestreak missile and the rear fuselage smoke-streaked from several orifices.

Wearing a partial pressure jerkin and anti-G trousers John Squier, English Electric's chief production test pilot, boards one of the pre-production Lightnings on 29 September 1959. Next day he made the world's fastest supersonic ejection when his Lightning T4 prototype, XL628, became uncontrollable at Mach 1.7 (some 1,200 mph) and 40,000ft. He fell into the sea. After air-sea rescue efforts failed to find him and it was believed he had not survived, he paddled ashore in his dinghy twenty-eight hours later.

Built as a Lightning T4, XM967 was converted to a T5 by BAC Filton and first got airborne on 30 March 1962. Flown on trials by English Electric, BAC, A&AEE and RAE Farnborough, it was earmarked for preservation but was scrapped in July 1976.

A Lightning F3A born and bred. When it was eighteen months old this aircraft was converted to full F6 standard. Here it spares a few moments during a test flight to be photographed, not at the end of Blackpool pier but in front of the world famous Tower.

The Lightning cockpit of the mid-1960s had the latest in primary flight instruments – some in different positions from those used for twenty-five years! The electronic Head-up Display had not yet arrived either.

January 1988. An all-grey Lightning T5 trainer (with Michael Gething, last aviation author to fly the Lightning, in the right-hand seat) with a camouflaged Lightning F6 XR771. Both aircraft belonged to RAF Binbrook's No.11 Squadron.

The same Lightning F6 displays its arrow-head plan view, two Red Top air-to-air missiles and its slightly off-set flight refuelling boom ...

... which it is about to stuff up the cone-shaped basket on the end of the hose reeled out from the VC10K3, ZA148 of No.101 Squadron up from RAF Brize Norton, Oxfordshire.

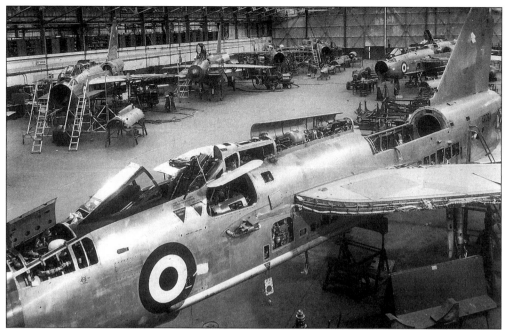

Lightning production. The nearest aircraft, XR764, was built as an F3A in 1965 but was converted to an F6. Not even a Blackpool fortune-teller could have forecast that, on 30 July 1971, it would fall flaming into Limasol Bay, Cyprus after the pilot had banged out.

Mainly for modellers. This Lightning F6, XS903, reveals details of the hot end of its Red Top missiles, over-wing tanks, ventral pod, Matra under-wing rocket pod and Dowty skewed-axis main landing gear.

A multi-role Lightning F6 with twin rocket pods on under-wing pylons, stands proudly behind some of the ordnance it can carry. Is that pitot head boom *really* bent?

Lightning All-Sorts. From the top; A T55 two-seater for Kuwait; F53, 53-686, for Royal Saudi Air Force (which appeared in the 1968 SBAC Farnborough Show with Class B markings G-AWON) and here carries a ventral gun pack; Lightning F6, XR759, converted from a F3A.

In 1966 orders for Lightnings from Saudi Arabia were hot news. BAC smartly put Saudi Arabian Air Force markings on an F6, XR770, and whizzed it off to the Farnborough Air Display where it is shown here waiting on the main runway for take-off.

When Saudi Arabia wanted Lightning two-seat trainers ASAP, two ex-RAF T4s (XM989 and XM992) were converted during April-June 1966 to become these T54s serialled 54-650 and 54-651 respectively.

This Lightning F53, based on the F6, was the first of a dozen exported to Kuwait during 1968-1969. In addition to its Arabic serial number it carries British Class B registration G27-80.

TSR.2 ready for final painting

Six

Combined Operations

By August 1962 work on the exciting TSR.2 had begun. The part 'ship-sets' of sub-assemblies for the prototype built at Weybridge by Vickers and at Warton went to the A&AEE, Boscombe Down for final assembly. The first flight of the first prototype, XR219, came on 27 September 1964. Beamont was pilot with Donald Bowen as chief test navigator. This was the only TSR.2 to fly. It made twenty-four flights before the entire programme was cancelled on 6 April 1965 with the order that all existing jigs, tools and airframe components should be broken up. This political decision was a great blow to BAC and its employees. However, another political decision, taken in collaboration with France, led to the joint design and manufacture of the Jaguar tactical fighter and trainer with production lines in both countries. BAC (Preston Division) was the British partner in this Anglo-French programme. A joint production plan for an Anglo-French variable-geometry aeroplane ended when the French pulled out; however, preliminary studies of swing-wing aircraft (the popular term for 'variable geometry') led to the tri-national Multi-Role Combat Aircraft (MRCA), later named Tornado. (Some newspapers still refer to this aeroplane as 'the multi-roll fighter'! One is tempted to ask 'Sausage, cheese or Swiss?'). Britain, West Germany and Italy collaborated in this great programme and Panavia Aircraft GmbH was created to co-ordinate all its commercial and manufacturing elements. The three partners in Panavia are BAC, MBB and Aeritalia. Currently nearly 1,000 Tornados have been assembled in the UK, Germany and Italy, using major sub-sections produced in the three countries, for the RAF, *Luftwaffe* and *Marineflieger*, *Aeronautica Militare Italiana* and the Royal Saudi Air Force. Of these 518 have been assembled at Warton. The first Warton-built MRCA was flown by Paul Millett, BAC Military Aircraft Division's chief test pilot, on 30 October 1974. By that time the Company had undergone another re-organisation with the nationalisation of the British aircraft industry. From 1 January 1978 it was British Aerospace (Military Aircraft Division) then became British Aerospace Defence (Military Aircraft). In September 1998 it answered to the call 'British Aerospace (Military Aircraft and Aerostructures)'. At the end of that year Tornados equipped sixteen RAF squadrons and five other Units.

Other aircraft built and assembled by the Division at Warton were the Jet Provost Mk5 trainer, the Strikemaster, its militarised export variant as well as some 140 single and two seat Hawks. Also built there was the EAP, the Experimental Aircraft Programme's Technology Demonstrator aircraft that led to the Eurofighter Typhoon with which the Division is currently involved. A major task is the Mid-Life-Update of some 140 Tornado Mks GR1/GR1As. The RAF began receiving updated aircraft in November 1997 and the programme should be completed by November 2002. A task confirmed in August 1998 stems from the upgrading of the Jaguar's Adour turbo-fan engine. This new power unit will be developed, manufactured and supplied by Rolls-Royce. British Aerospace at Warton has responsibility for designing, integrating and flight-testing the re-engined Jaguars whose operational life will be extended until about 2008. At the end of 1998 Nos 6, 41 and 54 Squadrons and the Operational Conversion Unit still operated Jaguars.

At the time of writing, the Division's fleet of ten Tornados, five Hawks and two Eurofighter Typhoons were heavily involved with development flying at Warton. This latter aircraft is being built by British Aerospace in collaboration with Alenia in Italy, Construcciones Aeronauticas SA (CASA) in Spain and Germany's Daimler-Benz Aerospace (DASA). These companies own Eurofighter GmbH which was set up to manage development of the complete aircraft. Britain has a 37% share of the work involved.

In September 1998 British Aerospace (Military Aircraft and Aerostructures) announced that machining of the first major Eurofighter components had begun at Samlesbury. These centre fuselage assembly frames were the first production 'flying' components to be delivered to DASA in Bremen. BAe invested some £21 million to provide world class, high-tech, tooling facilities and a machining system at Samlesbury as well as training for their operators. A total of 620 aircraft are to be built initially with delivery of the first of 232 to the Royal Air Force planned to begin in 2002.

While national and multi-national Defence programmes are still political footballs which can be 'kicked into touch' by any of the participants, the Eurofighter programme appears to offer a greater degree of stability and permanence than some others. Thus, the Warton/Samlesbury aeroplane-creating facilities (if that's not a too pompous way of saying 'factories') and their workforces seem to have security of employment for many years ahead. End of story – so far.

The prototype TSR.2 at Vickers-Armstrong's Weybridge factory revealing the long nose, small one-piece wing with 60° leading edge sweep and anhedral tips. Behind it the second TSR.2 is being assembled.

Like the back of a bus! The camera has converted the sleek shape of the TSR.2 into a blunt-nosed bustle-bottomed monstrosity with a tail plane almost as big as its wing.

On the golden afternoon of Sunday, 27 September 1964 the first all-white TSR.2 gets airborne for the first time at Boscombe Down. Aboard were Roly Beamont and the chief test navigator Don Bowen. The flight lasted fourteen minutes. 'This looks like being a real winner' said Beamont.

Some 3,000 Warton employees turned out to see the TSR.2 arrive back 'home' on 22 February 1965 after it had exceeded Mach 1.0 for the first time during the flight.

The TSR.2 in flight. Free from excrescences this beautiful aeroplane was a remarkably clean aerodynamic shape that helped to provide a smooth ride for crew and equipment at all speeds.

Three Warton winners. Photographed in 1965 are Canberra B.2, WD937, Lightning F.6, XR759 which was scrapped in April 1988 having logged 3,748 flying hours and TSR.2, XR219.

Some members of the TSR.2 design team line up for a farewell photograph in 1965.

The prototype of the BAC 167 – later Strikemaster – first flew on 26 October 1967. Developed from the Jet Provost 5 as a light attack/trainer aircraft, substantial numbers of both types were built at Warton for the RAF and for export.

Jaguar production in No.4 Hangar at Warton – which appears to be in the hands of seven 'workers' with one standing guard!

Jaguar XX765 was the test vehicle for British Aerospace's Active Control Technology research programme.

The same Jaguar with LERX (leading edge root extension) wing flies back to Warton from the 1984 Farnborough Show with the third production Tornado ADV ZD901. In 1988 this Jaguar became the world's first aircraft to fly with an all-digital Quadruplex fly-by-wire control system.

This Jaguar GR1 from No. 6 Squadron based at RAF Coltishall is armed with Sidewinder AIM9L self-defence missiles on its outboard under-wing pylons.

Chris Yeo, Warton's Jaguar project pilot, flies a Jaguar International S single-seater (top) in 1979 while deputy chief test pilot Tim Ferguson shares the two-seat trainer B version with Wing Commander D.R. Nadkarni, OC of No.14 Squadron, Indian Air Force, the first to fly Jaguars.

This British prototype multi-role combat aircraft (MRCA) P02 is being first flown on 30 October 1974 at Warton by Paul Millett, BAC Military Aircraft Division's chief test pilot, with Pietro Trevisan, Aeritalia's MRCA project pilot in the rear seat.

The white and red MRCA P02, XX946, with the reheat wicks turned up, creates a small vapour cloud over the partially swept wings. Note the 'pen-nib' shape of the spine under the rudder.

A later flight by the second prototype of the tri-national Panavia MRCA P02 built by BAC at Warton, Messerschmitt-Bolkow-Blohm in Germany and Italy's Aeritalia. The spine under the rudder has been restyled.

MRCA P02, with wings swept 67°, carries two 330gallon drop-tanks on under-fuselage pylons.

The first flight of the second British MRCA, PO3, XX947, on 5 August 1975. This was the first to have dual controls. David Eagles, BAC's MRCA project pilot, flew it with Tim Ferguson in the second seat.

MRCA PO3 on one of the eleven test flights it made from Warton in four days during August 1975. Note the flexible seal webs over the fuselage 'pockets' into which the wing's trailing edge slides when swept back.

MRCA PO3 takes-off from Warton in 'a typical long range, low-level strike configuration'. It hefts eight 1,000lb bombs, two full 330gallon fuel-tanks and two electronic counter-measures pods. Total take-off weight is twenty-six tons.

Panavia Standards Committee's 50th meeting, 16-18 March 1976. Present were J. Wilcock (chairman), S. Bentley (secretary), Constatin Valli, P. Morris, F. Gamble, K. Meyr, U. Klaus, F. Turlock, R. Knight, B. Barbonardin, J. Hind, S. Cooper, G. Hoffman, J. Eller, J. Foley.

A fine aerial view of the Strand Road, Preston Site seen during the late 1970s. The company still occupied part of the factory.

British MRCA markings were complex. Tri-national roundel nose port side; RAF roundel starboard nose and both sides of fin; German iron cross above and below starboard wing and Italian roundels on port wing. German and Italian MRCAs' markings were different!

Tornado GR1, ZA462/EM, one of Production Batch Three of sixty-eight British aircraft ordered in June 1979. It first flew on 29 July 1983 and joined No.15 Squadron at Laarbruch, West Germany in February 1984.

First take-off of ZA254, the white and black first Tornado F2 ADV (air defence variant) on 27 October 1979. The pilot was David Eagles with Warton's Roy Kenward, ADV project navigator. During the very long ninety-two minute first flight it achieved Mach 1.2. It carries four Skyflash under-fuselage missiles and two Sidewinders

This unusual underneath view of the first Tornado ADV shows it carrying four Skyflash missiles plus a single Sidewinder and two 330 gallon fuel tanks on the inboard wing pylons.

A Skyflash missile is fired from a Frazer-Nash launcher under the second Tornado F2, ZA267 during November 1981. It was flown on various trials by A&AEE, Boscombe Down.

Tornado ADV loaded with four Skyflash missiles, a pair of Sidewinders and a couple of drop tanks banks away from the open rear doors of an RAF Hercules and the photographer.

Warton's Design Office Standards Group in April 1982. From left; Andrew Wilson, Jack Wilcock (group leader), John Hind, Sydney Butler, Ian McCormack, Joyce Bradburn, Maurice Roe, David Britten, Sandra Cooper, Harry Bentley, Felix Leaver, Peter Morris.

ZE162/AY, a missile-laden Tornado F3 of No.229 Operational Conversion Unit based at Coningsby climbs steeply in company with the photographic aircraft.

No.29 Squadron Tornado F3s carry the Roman numerals XXX (30) on their air intakes. A probably apocryphal 1920s story relates that a Sergeant told an airman "Paint the Squadron number in Roman numerals on that Grebe. Do two exes, then one exe" i.e. XXIX. Following instructions the airman painted two exes - XX, then one exe - X. Result ? XXX!

A No.29 Squadron Tornado F3, ZE288/BI, and a Royal Malaysian Air Force Northrop F-5E Tiger Eye seen at Butterworth, western Malaysia, during Air Defence Exercise Lima Bersatu in September 1988.

In the late 1970s the project design team at British Aerospace, Warton, had produced studies for a new fighter looking very much like the Experimental Aircraft Programme demonstrator aircraft that would fly a decade into the future. Before that there were many alternative designs. This was just one of them.

On 13 June 1984 a dismantled tatty Spitfire PRXIX, PS915, arrived at No.4 Shed, Samlesbury for restoration. Discussing the project at Strand Road are, clockwise from left; John Waite, technical manager Tornado development (Spitfire project co-ordinator); David Eagles, executive director, flight operations; Air Vice Marshal Kenneth Hayr, Air Officer Commanding No.11 Group, RAF Strike Command and Frank Roe, managing director.

Some of the Spitfire project team of technical instructors, craftsmen and apprentices at British Aerospace Samlesbury who were involved with this great two-year restoration programme.

Warton, 27 October 1985. The EAP was nearing completion when it was removed from the assembly hangar for calibration tests.

The completed EAP, shown a few weeks before its first flight at Warton on 8 August 1986. The canard control surfaces and split air-intake are notable features.

Farnborough, September 1986. Before a vast, expectant crowd, ZF534, the EAP demonstrator in its white and blue livery, taxies to its take-off point....

.... reaches it, turns and noses into wind ....

.... gets airborne very rapidly, tucks up its landing gear....

.... and climbs away, with reheat fires lit in the two jet pipes, to commence its stunning display of agile flying.

On 16 December 1986 Squadron Leader Paul Day from the RAF Battle of Britain Memorial Flight took the now resplendent Spitfire PRXIX into the air for the first time for twenty-nine years.

The British-built second development Eurofighter Typhoon, ZH588, that first flew on 6 April 1994 at Warton.

Eurofighter development aircraft DA2 with the two-seat DA4, ZH590, at high altitude in the sun. The trainer, which first flew on 14 March 1998, is also a fully operational aircraft.

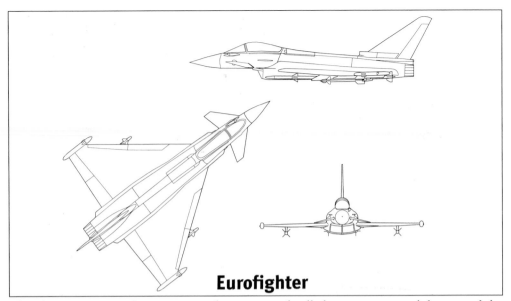

Eurofighter

This three-view general arrangement drawing reveals all the major external features of the Eurofighter Typhoon.

Four months after the Eurofighter first flew, an airship photographed the demolition work on the historic site at Strand Road, Preston. *Sic transit gloria mundi*.